DEVELOPING A PHOTOGRAPH OF GOD

Developing a Photograph of God
Copyright © 2014 Robert S. King
Paperback ISBN: 978-0-9840352-6-7

All rights reserved: except for the purpose of quoting brief passages for review, no part of this book may be reproduced or transmitted in any form or by any means, electronic or mechanical, including photocopying, recording, or by any information storage and retrieval system, without permission in writing from the publisher.

Cover art: Mauro Bighin | Dreamstime.com
Cover design: Steven Asmussen
Design & Layout: Steven Asmussen

Glass Lyre Press, LLC.
P.O. Box 2693
Glenview, IL 60026

www.GlassLyrePress.com

Developing a Photograph of God

Poems by
Robert S. King

Foreword

Developing a Photograph of God by Robert S. King is a wonderfully cohesive and morally serious examination of the topic he evokes in the poem *When the Road Curves Back* "to find out why I'm here."

There are four sections. In the first, **The God Particles**, King tells us "We auction our lives who never question God" (Asking God to Change) and he ruminates "Maybe the spirit needs to hide / behind something that matters" (Spiritual Matters).

In the second section, **How to Kill the Soul**, King explores the vanities of our lives. Camping in a late Fall Forest says, "Our camouflage has faded but not the stains where we last touched." He portrays human insularity in Wall Street, picturing walkers on cell phones "full of clang and clatter… mute voices inside moving barrels."

The third section, **A Darkroom of Old Negatives**, addresses age and loss: "If old age is closer to God / why do my photos curl up and fade (Where it Aches Most).

The fourth section, The God of Infinity & Zero, is one of resolution in which King comes to grips with the singular questions of our shared humanity. In Snowflakes on a Hardening Land he begins, "I am tired of beauty," but concludes "In hard times, touch must be the vision." From the Chrysalis looks back, "If only I could spread it all out again," and forward to "a short flight to heaven / or at least to absolute zero." In Drinking at the Spotlight's Well he says, "our dark eyes adjust/to the possibilities of brilliance."

The final poem, A Window on the Best of Impossibilities, investigates string theory to tell us "No string of any world is a loose end / the stars tell their stories in winks."

This collection engages the 'dark night of the soul' and the presumptions of optimism: that life has meaning as King says in the last poem "that my small telescope can pull both past / and future back to show me how far / the curious soul has traveled."

With a maturity of vision and a language drenched in lyric, King leaves us with remarkable images such as "Serpents of rain / puzzle of noise and clumsy dance," "the places / where regret nags, dreams freeze and hope crackles down in fire," and "Smell the feathers of the angels burning." These poems, intimate and agonized, swinging between the horns of hope and despair, shed illumination on the grave and haunting philosophical questions.

—**Joan Colby**, author of *Joan Colby: Selected Poems* and others

Contents

The God Particles
River Pulse	15
The Spirit of the Matter	16
How the Conscience Came to Be	17
Reinkarmation	18
Mother	20
Developing a Photograph of God	21
Eve Bares All She Knows	23
Cottonmouth Catchers in a Night Swamp	24
Voices from the Storm	25
Asking God to Change	26
The Children of Chaos	29
Explorer	30
Spiritual Matters	31

How to Kill the Soul
How to Kill the Soul	35
Camping in a Late Fall Forest	36
Wall Street	37
Downslide, Song of my Father	38
Something Missing	39
Orphan	40
Charity	41
Everlasting Life	42
How to Pay Respects to a Serial Killer	43
Appetites	44
Turtles Watching the Stars	45
How to Do Good When You're Dead	46
Harvesting the Impossible Dream	47
The Last Saint of the Empire	48
A Dutiful Ruler Speaks of Peace	49
Hero	50
Feeding the Body of Earth	51

A Darkroom of Old Negatives

Where It Aches Most	55
The New World Dictionary	56
Toasting a Dead Drinking Buddy	57
The Currents of Darkness	58
Wishing Well	59
Shadow Sharing	60
Shadow at Low Tide	61
Missing	62
Between Fire and Ice	63
Blending Time	64
The Old Poets Home	65
Prescriptions for Two	66
Old Storm	67
Reaching the Black Hole	68

The God of Infinity and Zero

Mechanics	73
Through the Membranes of Multiverses	74
Prophets Climbing to Machu Picchu	75
Where the Road Curves Back	76
Fishing the Blue Sky	77
For the Love of Roads	78
Snowflakes on a Hardening Land	79
Escape	80
The Places Most Remembered	81
From the Chrysalis	82
The Chrysalis of Coal	83
Built on Bones	84
Drinking at the Spotlight's Well	85
Gaia Elemental	86
A Window on the Best of Impossibilities	87

The God Particles

River Pulse

smoothed by wear
in any panned stream is a load of stones

call them eggs that never hatched

call one a heart too hard to break
that keeps the river flowing

The Spirit of the Matter

The heart of a stone is not cold.
Few know how deep is its touch,
how far its reach.

Few know of its cosmic voyage,
how we all connect by time and stardust.

The nearest sun warms it almost to glow.
Snow takes on its shape,
seems to melt into its heart.

Stones are the bones of all worlds.
The smooth one is an egg whose time
does not come until other beings feel its pulse.

Brighter than any bulb invented by man,
kinder than any vengeful God
hatched by fear and pride,
its yolk is the one true sun.

How the Conscience Came to Be

They used to call me an angel
before I advised God
to give his children knowledge
to grow better, to know better,
give them dreams of more than sex,
give them skills
to grow sweeter apples.

In eternal daylight, I sat
at God's table, eating Heaven's
ambrosia, laughing at His mighty jokes,
my feathers a uniform cleaned and pressed,
a yes-angel in the ear of the Lord.
No one at the company banquet questioned
the Know-It-All.

Finally I could no longer fold my wings
properly enough, could not hold
my serpent's tongue
forked but telling truth.

It was not God's truth.
It was not His creation.
It was He who fired me,
clipped my wings, threw me
to the molten core of earth.
But the voice of an angel
cannot be burned.

That is why today two voices whisper:
I in the left ear,
He in the right.

Reinkarmation

Never answer the boy
whose clock hands are question marks,
who asks, "have I been here before?"
Do not tell him these beach prints are his,
that they lead back to him,
where he became, where he'll become
an old man sailing off with nothing.
Do not tell how heaven refuses him again,
how his fingernails scream down another
tombstone, leaving no mark.

No, never name the young one.
He will have too many others to remember.
Do not say that the great waves
of time will wash him from shore to shore.
Do not let him know how his birthdays
count up then down, remember then forget,
as he stings from the bullet spray of an ocean
too deep for him or tosses in a sky
never higher than the crow's nest.

No, never let him see how the clock
strikes hard and repeats itself.

Instead, give him false hope.
Tell him how sails resemble angel wings,
but show him the danger of sailing
against the wind. Teach him that peace
is an island where only his memory can stay.

If he is like most, he'll turn the helm
the easy way toward a dream-lit shore
forgotten but familiar, stay afloat
through another life, numb and dumb
like a drunk on storming ocean,
laughing and swearing off the danger
until the next last day of his life.

Mother

—for Mildred Jones King, d. 1988, age 68

As long as I have a life, you have an afterlife.
Your ghost still remembers birthdays—
your breath blows out one candle at a time,
leaving me enough light for another dream
to come true. I still hear those days dawning—
you on the creaky floors, eggs sunny side up
and bacon popping, coffee pot grumbling,
biscuits rising early while the hoarse rooster
clears his throat in perfect weather.

Even today, your only hunger begs for more
than my black sheep's heart can give:
that I feed my soul with holy light
from He who gives more than expected back.

Mother, you've earned your rest.
Know that I seek communion in all of nature,
and my lack of faith is not a lack of virtue.
Know that my dark heart is just as true as yours,
and my rule is golden too. If there is a God
who made the rule, He surely declared
Let there be two of everything:
To understand the light,
one must know the darkness well.

Developing a Photograph of God

Evolution

You are sure the Hadron Collider will prove
in pictures that there is only one God particle.
You go by the Book, a scholar of shalt nots
and shalts. The top of your class,
you've grown to the tallest height allowed
and feel blessed to wed a girl named Faith.
You practice everything you preach
to little brothers looking up
and save the sinning mouths of debate class.

You obey the school dress code that narrows
your vision to a deeper understanding
as you pray inside the iron gate that holds all truth,
as you stroll bright halls whose bulbs are never
    changed.

It's a riddle that some dinosaur fossils have feathers,
but you'd like to lecture Darwin
that you've never seen birds laying raptor eggs.

So far you've taught Moses, your parrot,
a large vocabulary from the Old Testament.
That the bird knows *Jesus!* must be a miracle.

If more than one God particle shows on the picture,
which one will you obey?

Creation

With lab assistants named Google and Yahoo,
you search for a photograph of God,
some say to prove a negative.
You magnify microscopic galaxies
to find a theory of everything,
to prove the theory of your soul
is merely quantum energy and dying light.

Still it's a riddle how dark matter comes from
    nowhere,
though all God's children are bound by physical law.
Still it's a riddle how atoms disappear
but reappear when thought or sought.

If more than one God particle is caught on film,
which one will you follow?

Eve Bares All She Knows

I sing of the full moon hanging ripe on a limb.
I sing with my mouth full of fruit,
croon with the mockingbird a new tune
we cannot shake from our heads.

For a moment, the knowledge made me cold,
then taught me fire to tan my skin.
Before flames, I knew nothing of hell.
Before ash, I knew nothing of the future we cause.
Before fire, I knew nothing about the snake
between your legs that crawled into my cave.
I knew nothing of how my children will play with fire.

Now we both know that life burns us alive,
know the bitter aftertaste of sweet fruit's ash,
hear strange passions blowing around us,
flutes of hollow trees played by wind, a voice
rising from the snake or God—
which one we cannot always tell.

We cannot keep the secrets of creation
and destruction to ourselves. The whole world knows
us now, as we know it. Now we hide nakedness
in the lie of a new dress code.
All of this owed to taking a bite of the moon!
All of this owed to our Lord keeping secrets from us!
Is He not to blame as well?

Neither God nor snake lied.
How can we know who is more true?
Love, let's strip down to the flesh and start again.
Like angels, let's bloom feathers from our shoulder blades
and fly to another paradise. Let the tears
that fall from our knowledge nourish our garden well.

Cottonmouth Catchers in a Night Swamp

The trick is to charm its bobbing head with light.
Make the devil stare till he's blind,
and while your flimsy lifeboat crawls
toward the other bank,
let your own arm become a snake,
coil back with your right hand open
like a pure mouth capable of swallowing
something bigger than itself.

Let your arm strike as a strangler,
clamp the serpent just below the head,
cram this ancient sinner in a bag.

Now row back to sunrise,
milk him for all he's worth,
keep him charmed with living light,
never showing him your shadow,
your black spot,
your bullseye.

Voices from the Storm

Rain strikes down with a hissing of snakes,
splashes up as shards of my mirror,
so loud I cannot hear the future breaking.
The storm in my head is blowing
fragile dancers apart, a universe
of pieces expanding.

Even on clear nights, glass stars
rain down in shatter. Feathers fall
like rocks and old apples full of holes.
Doors slam through the hallways of covered ears.
A lost wind tears itself into four directions,
each whispering a secret to a wormhole.

I piece back a jigsaw image in the glass,
facing myself too close for comfort.
In the loud storm of my life, I cannot hear
my own thoughts or read my lips, but I'll listen
to the end for the greater voice singing
in the calm eye of the storm, giving melody
and meaning to these serpents of rain,
to this puzzle of noise and clumsy dance.

Asking God to Change

I. Honk If You're Guilty

On the raucous road to hell or heaven,
everyone stands trial. A black sheep,
I pled *not sure*, and the judge hammered
my life in contempt because uncertainty
is not piety. So I drew my own map
of the world, removed all the borders,
erased the points of power.

But there were too many holy roads to repave
and too many signs I could not argue
with along the way. I got no answer
when I asked a Yield sign *why*?

Signs save lives, they say. I say they
herd the flock toward a final shearing.
Ahead is a toll gate run by hawks without change.
Ahead is the chicken of my last meal
and the vulture with its ear to my heart.

II. Saying Grace

I am too curious a man.
I no longer see myself in the mirror
because I have asked all the questions
I can answer. So I pray to the wind
and stars, hoping they know
why life and death belong to the same
vicious circle, why they are just different
sides of the same coin and have the same
value—the sum of nothing more
than profit and loss—why everything
has a price, why the fuel of every creature
is the daily killing and eating of other life.

Star scholars say everything of matter
is made of stardust.
Then we are all cannibals, I say.

Death nourishes life, but pray for this truth
to change. Pray we are God as God is us.
We are in this together, and it matters not
if truth is God or Science,
nor which one Nature obeys.

III. Allowing Food in the Courtroom

My development was arrested,
my path to knowledge brought before the judge.

Crossroads are illusions. The path
is a straight line or a circle, both leading
to an end or another circle.
Only curiosity can fly in any direction,
but there is a price to pay for even one question.
I hurl a prayer, a shot into the dark of space.
I hear its Doppler shift of wheels and hooves
stampeding around a black hole
that swallows it whole.

Can a simple question reshape the mind of God,
give Nature food for thought?
I pray that knowledge is our food,
I pray we hunger for light to a better way.
I pray we never get comfortable in our skins,
that our God will consider shedding his own.

We who never change make God old and set in his ways.
We auction our lives who never question God.
Too late, now my long silence hears the gavel
sentencing me to life without control.

The Children of Chaos

I lived here on earth
long before I was born.

Nothing anywhere is native,
but everything belongs.
Past, present, and future coexist,
but nothing stays the same.
Under the electron microscope,
everything is a scatter of matter,
the small universe as vast
as its larger self. Yet distance
somehow warps: Through any scope
everything is a matter of importance
that explodes, collides, merges—super
novae and black holes stirred in a soup
rising to the boil of another journey,
attracted by the gravity of elsewhere.

Pieces of the greater mind bang about,
looking for the one who bore them.

Explorer

Wind imposes its will
in my moth-eaten but seaworthy sail.
On an ocean of sorrow and regret,
the gales of hope and fear howl
together toward an unknown shore.

How far can I see from the crow's nest
without knowing how many wings and fins
have drowned in the soul's dark depths?
Waves from the island of my life
come back again and again
across the bow of vision.

The short lives that orbit light
stream like moths navigating
the dark, sailing upwards
toward the warm light of stars,
going through bright holes
they've chewed in the fabric of darkness.

Spiritual Matters

I itch to know what makes the soul
join so little as the flesh,
wiring itself to raw nerves,
pounded by the heart
and groans of the groin.

If only I could dissect myself,
my atoms, quarks, and strings,
down to the God particle,
maybe I'd know why
the universe flies apart,
know what galactic arms
are strong enough to hold
even pieces of nothing together.

Maybe the spirit needs to hide
behind something that matters.
Maybe the body needs
its spirit's lightning.

Perhaps the soul does not exist.
Perhaps matter does not matter.

How to Kill the Soul

How to Kill the Soul

Aim for the heart
of stone or gold. Aim
for the hollow heart.

Every soul has one.

When the soul dies it lives
for power. Its ghost could
rule the world.

Camping in a Late Fall Forest

This land owns forever
what it breaks apart, will not
let go, though limbs crack in pain.
Grown rough as bark, our hands
have not built a home in heaven
where the land holds firm.

Wind tears holes in the tent
that never keeps us warm.
Leaves rattle like brittle bones
as they try to fly off with late birds.
Everything loose is leaving.
Only the roots remain like memories
of fruit trees we thought we'd plant
in some better season.

Our camouflage has faded
but not the stains where we last touched.
Then the tent flies off; only the stakes remain.
Exposed now, we shiver beneath
a white blanket, our fire
shrinking beneath the snow.

We keep low to the ground like roots,
determined to outlast this winter
where nothing grows but distance.

Wall Street

With cell phones like pacemakers
for artificial hearts, each day
the same pulses blip along worn
winter sidewalks. Faces in scarves and collars
come and go, avoiding eyes, daydreaming
their way farther each day
from where they have to go.

Walking with heads bowed to feet,
they seem no more than silence and shoes,
bubbles of solitude in circles of secrets.
Neither honks nor jackhammers break the ice
of tin men hollow at the heart, full of clang
and clatter disguising the emptiness inside,
muted voices in moving barrels hearing only
the hollow echoes of their last words.

Downslide, Song of my Father

—for B. N. King, Guitarist and Clockmaker, d.2006, almost 88

Songs old and body brittle, any raindrop
might break his bones. He cannot stop
the shrinking of skin on bone, the wasting away.
His heart weighs more of monolith each day.
Even his guitar cannot pick away the blues,
nor can time his many ticking clocks defuse.

His life is clear as mud tracked in from rain;
every trace of his old self leaves a stain
and footprints deep as graves. He in pits
deeper than he is high, never quits,
though it takes an ever greater toll
to climb out of ever deeper holes.

Something Missing

He leans out of a tenth-story window,
but no one below bets he'll jump.
There is no melodramatic ledge or stage
for his farewell performance,
so mothers let their children watch.

His cigarette cinders float
gently down, as if he were scattering
his own ashes, as if he too could
glide softer than any working stiff
to the hard concrete life below.
He gives the shirt off his back
to the wind, the parachute
opening into a skull of half a mind.
It would take binoculars to prove
his public nakedness.

Only when he drapes a leg
over the sill do some start to clap.
Even then only the addicts place bets.
Most of us won't stay for the last act;
Live News will tell us
if we missed anything.

Orphan

The child in a man's body
moves every day to a different
cardboard house, never sleeps
in the Shelter, that orphanage
for grown-ups.

His mouth is always open,
a hollow ring, a silent shout,
the calm before the storm.

They call him Stormy,
this child who refused
his unadopted name.
Hard rain named him.
No tears now, but years
leak in, leak out.

He was never anyone's,
never at home, lives everywhere.
His stare seems to follow
some distant sound,
some wandering echo
seeking the voice that made it.

Charity

My snowprints reach a woodland home
fenced in by clouds and icicle limbs,
a house of brick and window light,
an insulated bubble in the darkness.

Surely, warmth glows inside every room.
What light leaks out is charity
to snowdrift strangers like me.

Would my knock on the door put the lights out,
set off the dog alarm? Would I hear
feet and voices tangling up in a cold rush to quiet?

Warm homes have acted that way before.

Everlasting Life

Now in the whiskered mirror of manhood
I recall how the same hymn always played out
into the pews, how the sweating preacher
summoned the frightened boy in me
to come forth, be saved, be reborn
into the long, loving arms of Jesus.

Too young to run, too old to hide,
bound to the inquisition,
my congregation sang be one of it,
though I never fit into the halo
they tightened on my head.
The pressure burned my brow
like a spotlight of thorns, and I sang off-key
like a bitten bird in the cat's mouth.

So in the land where good
boys clean their plates,
pledge allegiance, go to war
for any reason given,
I stepped in sweat and tears to the altar,
was wrapped in hugs of salvation,
gave witness, imitated the testimony
of so many saved souls before me, amen,
about the peace and love I felt, amen,
about my 12-year-old sins, amen,
and how now I'd walk in his light forever, amen…

And today in broad daylight I killed a man
who looked like Jesus.

How to Pay Respects to a Serial Killer

A funeral director must have
a way with words that sound
more like silence.
Undertaking is an art form
that shaves the blood-stained beard
of the honored beast
so that the eulogist may outline
his good points to explain why God
allowed a monster among us.

Remember, both mourners and celebrants
would rather be home with martinis.
Don't frown, but a sympathetic smile
will ensure repeat business.
Today, especially,
keep the service short.

Follow the script and the scripture.
Even the biography of the damned
is told with sobbing compassion.
In the case of a killer, stretch the tales
of good deeds as far as possible,
whispering priest and rabbi jokes as filler.
Deliver his death with rose petals,
sweeter scented than any twisted
life whose sins are left unspoken
on this his only day of tribute.

Know your audience.
Though so many pour out,
no one dare say
that these are tears of joy.

Appetites

Carrot biters or flesh predators,
everyone eats corpses every day.
Animal lovers, saints who don't
eat meat, feast on bodies
once buried in garden rows.
All children of nature learn
to consume beyond remorse.

If we ponder the murders,
hear the wailing ghosts
of beasts and fruits, our hearts
might break like mirrors.
Perhaps then we'd rather starve
or eat ourselves
than take another life.

Turtles Watching the Stars

Some say our eyes make everything smaller
like looking down the wrong end of a telescope
where watery lights of stars swim
at the top of a well,
light years away but liquid as dream,
reflective bubbles orbiting far above
our shell-shocked past.

We do not want outsiders close
enough to touch,
just close enough to dream of,
where our own sky is the limit.
Their shells explode against ours,
barely heard.

We seldom make a move
in our mobile homes,
in our private pleasure domes,
and the scenery is better in oblivion
and in dream.

We never magnify.
We only multiply slowly,
and none from our eggs will fly.

We're old soldiers cowering under helmets,
gazing at the static heavens
on the ceilings of our shells.

How to Do Good When You're Dead

You'll have to do magic as a ghost,
not fully dead or alive but dangerous.

Money no longer counts. Make
its disciples count their blessings instead.

Learn their illusions. Practice in mirrors
where the rich admire their worth.

Do your disappearing act.
Haunt the greedy. Scare them straight.

Steal their identities, then expose yourself
as you have exposed them.

Whisper in their ears, softly like pickpockets,
that you live in their hidden pockets and vaults.

Blow kisses and all their paper money
down the streets of the poor.

Harvesting the Impossible Dream

While we warm one side of ourselves
around the fire barrel, while red
flashing lights and yellow tape ban us
and guns bark back and forth,
the sky we've prayed to drops
its diamonds in the sparkling grass
of dawn, manna to fill our eyes
if not our empty bellies.

We rise up from the long, cold,
bedless night where the diamonds
used to wink above us out of reach.
We harvest them now on earth
in the old fields of our labors
where everything done to us
is dimming scarshine,
where everything we have done
shines for the taking.

The Last Saint of the Empire

Stranger, I am cupping in my hands
the land's last water for you.
You will not drink alone.
The sun too is steaming in this meager pool.

Drink before the water boils away.

What you have won is mostly smoke:
Above us, old mystics, old clouds,
redden from the dust of battle:
the wind twists them like sponges,
wringing out across the valley
a dry and crimson rain:
Even the gentle, holy winds rub
together like flint:
below them the frocks flame:
the shadows of monks are dark ash
piling up in prayer.

My invader, my wounded heir,
you are drinking my boiling blood.
You must swallow what you conquer.
You must dress for the weather you bring.

It is a hot day:
Smell the feathers of the angels burning.

A Dutiful Ruler Speaks of Peace

The mirror of the reflecting pool sweats.
Steam rises, curls like a burial gown
into Lincoln's carved lap.

My own sweat is the nation's water supply,
its holy water, a well I've poisoned as well
as those before me, where the wind howls lies
told on so many cold inauguration days,
where truth flees from fists and flags raised
in the blinding fireworks of July.

The blood of my father and children is spoiled,
a green counterfeit I've spilled around the world,
a cultural hemlock I've forced all peoples to drink
even on this Independence Day.

Why not repeat history?
What else can a nation born of war do?
My lady in the harbor carries a torch
to light the battle fire.

The tanks and troops parade by;
the jets whistle above like birds,
rockets like hawks spread contrails
feathery as American dreams.
These are my arms reaching out to the world.

Hero

After so many have gone to seed,
I am almost a whole nation now.
I am the last legend with a leg to stand on
as the war whimpers down, the most
upright in a field of blackened bodies.
Victory settles who is right.

Then why am I still burning?
Why does smoke still rise
from the chests of enemies I killed long ago?
Why does this smoke follow me,
cloud my mirror, choke my peace of mind?

Am I done too, cooked from the inside
like Hiroshima's glowing remains?
I have made it home to be an oak,
to stand on guard to protect my land;
I have sucked the air from all danger,
snuffed the spread of any blaze,
except for my own leaves still falling,
my own limbs forever popping down in fire.

Feeding the Body of Earth

if one of us who were cloven to bits
could remember the forest our body on our journey
if one of us could feel the forest sleeping
in us on our stone pillows
then we'd awake all of us by a road
with our murderers in our arms

and we'd rock them in our arms
but one by one we dead fly out of our senses
one by one the tongue the nose the fingers the ears
would all of us forgive the battle for being long
and though the mortal wits fall in five separate fields
five decomposing memories
the wind is still a nerve between us
a spirit clearer than blood
that moves through the grass
to soothe amputated eyes
looking back at us between the blades

and their gaze might hold forever the last thing they saw:
the limbs lift an ax and hack the trunks down
or see each man a battlefield reclaimed by weeds

but there would swell an oak from every weed
there would shine new eyes in every nest
and one of us would be all of us
all our pieces in a gown of acid
one by one dissolving into the body of earth
one by one into the hues of its wings
one by one of us the crows would drop bits of us to their young
and all the roads our nerves would twitch and open wide

A Darkroom of Old Negatives

Where It Aches Most

If old age is closer to God,
why do my photos curl up and fade?
Why does He not shine the light for me
when I need Him most, show me
the old pictures in new light?

God's batteries must be dead.

Something throbs
between mind and muscle,
perhaps the aching soul that remains
when I take my last dose.

I'll hold my nose, open wide,
and take my medicine,
but it doesn't kill the pain
I want it to.

I see no path ahead,
only a dark waiting room
with spoons and bottles
labeled in fine print
no refills.

The New World Dictionary

Every word I've said has taken root,
grows the definitions of me—wildflower or
wildfire—
smokes from truth's fiercest battle
from whose barrel the best of me blooms,
or remains a scent, a possibility, a whisper
as leaf-rustle in a flock of thrashers
who know how they change color
before the fall.

Every word I've said has been uprooted,
a forget-me-not given rain but no light,
given to the wind of God's conscience,
around the small world
blowing things together, apart.

The same word wages war as powers peace:
desire, the stem of fire and flower.

Toasting a Dead Drinking Buddy

You never learned to drive,
never wanted to go anywhere
that didn't have a happy hour.

Even as a boy, you couldn't pedal
fast enough to balance left or right.
As a barfly man you never proposed,
but you charmed the ladies with free shots.
They called you Lightning Rod
because you were ten percent alcohol
with nerves of static electricity, because you
once burned down your tinderbox trailer
when you passed out with a burning Camel
between your fingers and the rug.

Even when you got burned by business
or booze, your scars could still charm
another day. A good job always
lasted long enough for a cold case
and a phone call for bail, or to invest
in some company for the night,
or to give my desperation your last dollar.

You never drove because Jack Daniels
quenched your thirst more than Texaco Hi-Test,
and you thought God shared your tastes
and protected drunks.

But finally you drove yourself into the ground.
Even then I thought you'd sleep it off
in heaven or hell, stagger back with an angel
at your side, your new drinking buddy.

The Currents of Darkness

Darkness is liquid,
is the temperature of swimmers
exploring cold depths
or sunning in the shallows.
When we shiver at the bottom,
our waves nudge lives
far beyond our vision.
When we sweat in the black water,
we fill its body like wind fills a sail.
With touch for rudder,
we flow like moths to a shore of light:
the long night turned inside out.

Wishing Well

The poor farm girl
sinks her pail deeply,
down to where the water
is most alive and flowing
over stream-polished stones.
It is most drinkable then,
far purer than her surface life
with its broken nails and backs,
long droughts of the heart,
and calloused hands.

She imagines diving in
to sleep in the living water,
at its deepest to float down
the underground river,
to revive on the soft skin
of a distant shore.

Shadow Sharing

Beneath a winter moon we share a dark coat,
each wrapped in a vow to keep the other
alive if not warm. The snow beneath
our feet drifts in white lies,
settles like eggshells to walk on.

Neither of us knows the way home.
We only know to keep our hands
in our pockets and to ourselves,
to stand near but not too close
to the campfire.

We both know the way to places we cannot go.
As the stars and moon like possibilities
hide behind the mountain,
we both know the places
where regret nags, dreams freeze,
and hope crackles down in fire.

Shadow at Low Tide

From the shore of a bad dream I watch
your lamp drift to sea, into the years
where you float, a flicker of colorful
light on the horizon.

You go down in flames with the sun,
and the only news of you comes back
in small waves shaped like hands
reaching out, pulling back, reaching back
into the memory where you are mist.
You did not promise to return,
but you swore you'd never sail away.

When the sea calms and gulls cry your name,
I think I hear you whisper on the breeze.
When the sea roils and lifeboats wash ashore
in splinters, I look for a message, a bottle.

No telescope can bring back the wind.
No one's love can make the wind circle forever
this deserted island. The wind blows all life
toward the other side. My last breath too
waits for its sails to fill. I fear it will not
bring me to your side.

How far did your wild hair sail?
The colors you left here faded with the tide.
I swim in the tear of our common water,
take comfort and sorrow in any shadow
shaped like you. I keep your memory
from fading like footprints washed away
from this shore where I am waiting, alone.

Missing

The older I get
the more I miss.

Midnight pepperoni once tasted
like passion instead of heartburn.
Legs went in the direction
I looked forward to,
and the weather was never cloudy
with cataracts.

Speed limits lower with age.
Life plays old jokes on us,
so I live in the past
where youth parties hard all night,
a past where the mind is bright but blank.

The younger I get
the less I miss.

Between Fire and Ice

In my old age
all pain is young,
is a child trapped
in a burning house
without doors.

The body is a stranger's
made of ice, cold
to the touch, fevered
by the old dreams
burning down.

Blending Time

Wrinkled skin
is a wrinkle in time.

I am old but also
rolling in dust
with puppy tongues.

I am young but also
rolling in a chair
to the end of a bright hall.

I am gone before
and gone after.
I've turned my back
and turned my head
to stir the senses
and tenses together:
stardust
in lasting light.

The Old Poets Home

The young have their metaphors too,
call us *geezers*, *crones*, and *loony tunes*;
say those old dude bards can't remember
their best pick-up lines, can't even
remember what they meant
to pick up.

Pardon my French, but *au contraire*.
Some of us can't forget
the old words finely polished
by the light from our eyes.
True, we read now to elderly ghosts
disappearing one by one from their seats,
mumbling like me who often loses his place.

But we stand by what we've said.
We've paid for our free verse
and still want the muse for lover,
though some say inspiration
has left us for someone younger.
Our children politely call
our aged metaphors *draft*.
Or did they say *daft*?

Prescriptions for Two

Months without surprise visits,
my companion is a pill large enough
to choke me but not the lungs' carcinoma.
Shall I take the prescribed drowsy hope
and nod away the day? Or shall I walk the floor,
wide awake with pain, with my lover,
the oxygen tank, in tow?

Either way, you stand behind me in a photograph.
Our bed sags on my side alone now.
A bookmark stays where you fell asleep.
A brush lies tangled up with your chemo hair.
The label says your last prescription just expired.
Your perfume makes me gasp with memory.

Like a snake I work the pill down my throat
and coil up into dream. May the knock at my door
come to take my breath away.

Old Storm

Another day of medicine and fog
when rain becomes reason enough
to drink beyond prescription.

Many clear days ago,
I rescued bottles washed up
on the beach—no messages within
or dose to take—just corks
holding in the last breaths of the dead.
I hoped they would whisper
what the other side is like.

I've taken too many baths on this side.
My skin shrinks in the water,
tighter each day. The top
of my head seems to be a roof
with a widening hole.

This could be the night
when the rain comes through,
washes up my empty lifeboat
on a distant shore, with only
a cork and bottle at the helm.

Reaching the Black Hole

I swim against the lowest point
of the whirlpool where the dead
surround me, circle the hole
in my life from which echoes respond
in vague, forgotten tongues.

The darkest self has only
liquid to hold onto,
a floating bottle as life jacket,
but a heart sinking like a rock.
The churn and whispers of tides
are a living pulse, but the stone
in my chest is barely beating.

Yet somewhere this spinning hole
has shore, lifeboat, lighthouse
with arms reaching out,
breaking through the glass surface
to free the heart's growth into thunder
sending new waves,
sailing a sudden message
in a bottle full of light.

The God of Infinity and Zero

Mechanics

An ache feels almost like a laugh,
a laugh much like a cry.
Cogs mesh in either direction.

Stardust in light merged
to make us all. Or was it shards
of dark matter striking each other,
sparking the light?

Pain and pleasure measure the same.
The length of a sigh gives voice to either.

Hurting together hurts less than apart.
Laughing together is more joy than alone.
Both grind down in the metal shavings of time,
mixed in the floor dust. Before the Big
Bang, God and Lucifer stirred together.

Whether Evolution creates or Creation evolves,
everything keeps time in the well-oiled clock
of God and Devil, Creature and Machine.
The gears turn in the one
mind of them all.

Through the Membranes of Multiverses

> *—Many scientists now theorize that there are multiple, even-parallel, universes like bubbles with membranes (aka branes) for borders*

Here without microscopic or telescopic vision,
I see nothing new, see my universe as a ghetto
of mortal flesh, yet feel billions of pulses
belonging all to one.

Often my mind swells and almost floats away,
but arms stretched to their limits
pull it back into the cramped cell of skull.
Blessed and cursed with curiosity, I have almost
gone out of my mind many times.

I wait for the day when arms fray
like ropes and snap loose, when the mind's *brane*
tears open and my little bang explodes
to the end of infinity.

Prophets Climbing to Machu Picchu

a seance blows from lower nights
and we glance back to flickering jewels
to see our eyes lying
like old stones
we lift them from our brother's grave

hurl them ahead to crown a silent mountain
hear them landing in a better time to wear them
       but they never settle they remember
       us falling
       us climbing the path with stones in our pockets
       brother brother step aside throw faster
       our eyes are rolling back to us

Where the Road Curves Back

In the deepest part of the curve,
you are on your knees in the middle of the road,
head bowed, hands cupping your face,
black gown blending into the asphalt,
a bouquet and empty bottle
cast off to the side of the road.

I stop two feet in front of you,
stagger out of the car with two headlights on,
as if they could shed any light on your story.

Only a memory could tell me why two lives
twist together in this curve
like two drunks who keep trying to dance.

I never know if your echo cries, laughs,
or repeats unanswered prayers.

I ask what is wrong. *To find out
is why I'm here* is your answer.

I ask to know your name. *To find out
is why I'm here* is your answer.

And both to find out and flee is why I go on
through nights bent double in this curve,
so warped that I almost meet myself coming back,
where in the leaving she shrinks
in my rearview mirror now,
where soon in another coming she will kneel
between my headlights again.

Fishing the Blue Sky

It seems a tall tale that I stop
precisely here at this sinkhole
full of water, this crater
in the middle of no one's road.
Is this a fishing hole or a mirror?
It seems all at once a mirage, a detour,
a choice I've made before.

I only know that the hole looks deep
in both directions and out of place
for one who follows a map.

I bend over and my eyes sink
to the bottom where swim
the big ones that got away.
There splash around and around
old failures abandoned
to the sinkhole of memory.

My eyes bob to the top to see
ripples of waves, reflections of clouds,
and the tops of trees spread out and flying.
This ceiling seems too high above me,
a sea without shoreline to guide.

When I was hooked on everyone's dream,
I never learned to catch fish that fit the pond,
was afraid to swim in the deepest waters.

Now I want to be a fish with wings,
a swimmer of the sky.
Today I choose a higher way of falling,
the way the wind blows,
the way I never traveled by.

For the Love of Roads

Moonlight paints the road's white lines.
Sometimes I travel with wind and rain
on ways unpaved, with mud for shoes,
past the warning barks of night
when doors are locked
and welcome mats worn out.

Like a shadow I pass by homes
haunted with darkness, hear voices
of those who will not let their light leak out
onto a road—while I stretch thinner, a seeker
who can never arrive or stay.

And when daylight shows my dangers,
I hurry past those who do not love a road,
whose arms are roots too short
to wrap around a wanderer's miles.
Only a glance reaches back to them
across the mountain's widening gap.
They are smoke fading from distant chimneys.

In dream, I've gone back home many times
but have never slept there well.
Drafts slam doors open and shut all night.
I take an open one that surely goes somewhere.

This way is not the one less traveled by,
but no vagabond can tell me which way to go.

Snowflakes on a Hardening Land

I am tired of beauty.
Its touch grows colder
across the landscape of lost dreams,
holding hostage the memory
of when beauty had a different face to tire of.
Winter grows harder each day,
and now I cannot see much beyond
the iceberg of my nose.

Fashion is fickle,
but now cold hearts are in style.
Everything wears a gown of snowflakes.
A beautiful snow-woman offers no warmth.
In this land, no snow-angels point the way to fire.
The flag stands guard, at stiff attention.

Lost in the blizzard, the river shivers and clots.
Empty nests fill with young snow.
Memories and eyes freeze shut.
Still, old hopes keep a small fire burning,
feel the face of beauty growing old,
then young, then old again.
In hard times, touch must be the vision
that senses clouds breaking,
the warm lighthouse of sun shining through.

Escape

I leave the walls to find a wilder life.
In the fantasy of a valley, I am first
to a river whose bubbles pop like fire,
whose cold currents shock all who touch
the flow, that sings of a dangerous paradise,
warning to keep the heavy off its back.

Yet wanderlusters and thrill-seekers
do not love a trail unblazed. They come.
They love the cold shock of waterslides.
Like bronco busters, they ride
waterfalls to the tamed pool below.

Too many come with boomboxes
louder than any waterfall. Forgive me
if I led them here to dam solitude's flow,
sail empty bottles and boxes down
the squirming back of the river,
whose misty spirit enslaves now
to the baggage of civilized wildlife like me,
like we who leave our scents in water
that could have quenched a purer soul.

Rapids clog and the river tries to fly,
to leap up from its weights and tangles.
Natives in feathered trees no longer sing
with the river whose voice chokes,
but they know why this ancient water
pushes so hard against its banks.

The Places Most Remembered

Perhaps I should sip cocktails on shores
where the muse surely skinny-dips
or nap in the beautiful lap of Mother Nature
who lullabies words and flowers
of sweetest meanings.
Maybe the hedonist in my head
will write these pleasures for you.

Or maybe the humanist in me
should stink like alleys breeding trash—
go down littered streets where hairless
boys dance with knives, play spin
the bottle with guns—go
into orphanages where small bodies
have large aching hearts.
Maybe my words should make holes
in this page, slouch their lines
from beauty toward the beast.

The best in me admires beauty from afar.
The beast's breath may come closest to art,
whose poem sucks loudest on the ears
from the wrong side of town.

From the Chrysalis

Zero is not as low as you can go.
I owe, therefore have less than nothing.
Wings of youth have turned to powder.

If only I could spread it all out again
as the colorful life of a butterfly
where wealth is a dance of beauty,
its wings painting a rainbow
on the wind, owing nothing, owning
nothing but time to dream
of a short flight to heaven—
or at least to absolute zero.

The Chrysalis of Coal

We poor go down into cold mines
in search of something to hold
light in our eyes.

Beams fold behind us into darkness.
Weather is a rain of dust and moths.

We cannot go back—
behind us the sound of downpour
and trapdoors slamming.

No matter, we say. We are moving on,
squeezing our pieces of coal
tighter than any womb.
We are listening to history,
listening for the future,
looking and longing
for a bright diamond light
on the tracks ahead.

For now hope flickers
in the flashlight.
Each footstep forward
leaves a story, a hole
where we pause to scratch arrows
on the walls for our rescuers.

We can hear time ticking
and cracking in both directions.
Even in black clouds of coal,
we can smell butterfly wings
turned to powder,
smell the crumbles
of who we almost are.

Built on Bones

       I have always lived by the laws of flesh
       shrinking tighter and shorter each hour.
       Now I've nothing to lose but cracking skin.
       Yet curiosity stretches wider, too strong an itch.
       In liquid imagination, I swan dive into
       the pool of my widest eye, splash down
       into the vast blue ocean of mind,
       wash my bones back to the civilized shore
       where those awaiting my last breath
       pick the marrow clean.

       On their solid beachhead, my skeleton
       has no heart, only a hard brotherhood
       where nothing more than hollow bones
       lean against one another
       and begin to crack.

Drinking at the Spotlight's Well

I never awaken from this ancient dream.
I walk through darkness to a circle of oldest trees.
In their center is a ghost of growth rings
in a hollow trunk full of star-bright water.
Around its roots, rocks kneel for communion.

Here is the place where the blind have visions,
drink holy water rained from a clearer world.
Intoxicated by the wine of hope,
stones warm and beat like hearts.
A lost lover's sudden kisses leave
small glowing moons on my cheeks.
Our dark eyes adjust
to the possibilities of brilliance,
and even the dead dance
in this living light.

Gaia Elemental

To wind that blows from better days
with the scent of mint and honeysuckle,
I thank you for this breath of fresh air
in weather long past prediction.

To sun that sets into the ocean
whose water does not dowse,
I warm my hands tonight
on the campfire you set today.

To rain that cleans and cools
the wounds and ends the thirsts
for more, from cupped hands I drink
my limit of clear waterfall.

To all that hungers,
all that aches from ice or fire,
may I learn to give what you need
and fair portion of what you want.

To the earth that bears us,
I mourn the scars of our legacy
but thank you for the home we share
atop your weathered body.

A Window on the Best of Impossibilities

> —*String Theory postulates that everything is made of vibrating, elastic strings*

Through the observatory lens stuck in my window,
my weak eyes reach out to landscapes
and starscapes beyond. I focus hard on the hope
that what I dream is seed to bloom on sky and land,
that my small telescope can pull both past
and future back to show me how far
the curious soul has traveled.

If I cannot see, I hope to hear the strings
vibrating through all of time and space.

If I cannot hear, I hope to see spiral galaxies
brushing their arms together in a painting of heaven,
so I or some starstruck creature worlds away
might find words to tie us all together.

No string of any world is a loose end.
The stars tell their stories in winks
and hide among storming clouds.
Still I vibrate with hope, wait for lightning,
and keep my window clean.

Acknowledgments

Grateful acknowledgments are made to the following publications in which many of these poems appeared, sometimes in earlier versions:

The Abstract Quill: "Escape"

Blue Lake Review: "Everlasting Life"

The Bookends Review: "Built on Bones"

Burningword: "Gaia Elemental"

The Chariton Review: "Feeding the Body of Earth"

Clarion: "Asking God to Change"

Construction: "Reinkarmation"

Dressing Room Poetry Journal: "Snowflakes on a Hardening Land"

East Coast Literary Review: "Voices from the Storm," "Mother," "Shadow Sharing"

ELF (Eclectic Literary Forum): "The New World Dictionary," "River Pulse"

En Passant: "The Last Saint of the Empire"

Eunoia Review: "Where the Road Curves Back," "The Chrysalis of Coal," "The Places Most Remembered," "Something Missing"

Gris-Gris: "Turtles Watching the Stars"

The Foliate Oak Literary Magazine: "Developing a Photograph of God"

Hobble Creek Review: "Charity"

The Lascaux Review: "How to Pay Respects to a Serial Killer"

Linden Avenue Literary Journal: "Shadow at Low Tide"

The Lullwater Review: "Prophets Climbing to Machu Picchu"

Metamorphosis: Writings About Aging (anthology, FutureCycle Press): "Prescriptions for Two"

The Mystic Nebula: "Reaching the Black Hole"

Northwind Magazine: "Hero," "Wishing Well"

Pirene's Fountain: "A Window on the Best of Impossibilities"

poeticdiversity: "Mechanics"

Requiem Magazine: "The Old Poets Home"

The Rufous City Review: "Camping in a Late Fall Forest"

Tiger's Eye Journal: "Old Storm"

The Tower Journal: "Appetites," "Between Fire and Ice," "The Children of Chaos," "Downslide, Song of My Father"

Viral Cat: "Spiritual Matters," "Drinking at the Spotlight's Well"

Wild Goose Poetry Review: "A Dutiful Ruler Speaks of Peace"

Writers' Forum: "Cottonmouth Catchers in a Night Swamp"

"River Pulse," "The New World Dictionary," "Cottonmouth Catchers in a Night Swamp," "Prophets Climbing to Machu Picchu," and "Last Saint of the Empire" are also reprinted from the author's previous book, *The Hunted River*, 2nd edition, FutureCycle Press, 2012.

"Feeding the Body of Earth" is also reprinted from the author's previous book, *The Gravedigger's Roots*, 2nd edition, FutureCycle Press 2012.

"Everlasting Life" is also reprinted from the author's previous book, *One Man's Profit*, Sweatshoppe Publications, 2013.

About the Author

Robert S. King, a native Georgian, now lives in Lexington, KY. His poems have appeared in hundreds of magazines, including *California Quarterly*, *Chariton Review*, *Hollins Critic*, *Kenyon Review*, *Main Street Rag*, *Midwest Quarterly*, *Negative Capability*, and *Southern Poetry Review*. He has published eight poetry collections, most recently *The Hunted River* and *The Gravedigger's Roots*, both in 2nd editions from FutureCycle Press, 2012; *One Man's Profit* from Sweatshoppe Publications, 2013; and *Diary of the Last Person on Earth* from Sybaritic Press, 2014. Robert is former director of FutureCycle Press and has served as editor/publisher of several presses.

GLASS LYRE PRESS, LLC
"Exceptional works to replenish the spirit"

Poetry collections
Poetry chapbooks
Select short & flash fiction
Occasional anthologies

Glass Lyre Press is a small independent literary press interested in work which is technically accomplished and distinctive in style, as well as fresh in its approach and treatment. Glass Lyre seeks writers of diverse backgrounds who display mastery over the many areas of contemporary literature: writers with a powerful and dynamic aesthetic, and ability to stir the imagination and engage the emotions and intellect of a wide audience of readers.

The Glass Lyre vision is to connect the world through language and art. We hope to expand the scope of poetry and short fiction for the general reader through exceptionally well-written books, which call forth our deepest emotions and thoughts, delight our senses, challenge our minds, and provide clarity, resonance and insight.

www.GlassLyrePress.com

www.ingramcontent.com/pod-product-compliance
Lightning Source LLC
Chambersburg PA
CBHW031300290426
44109CB00012B/653